Fabulous
Folded Flowers

CREATE 15 FLOWERS AND 5 ARRANGEMENTS

by Joost Langeveld
Book and Origami Papers Designed by Kyung-Ah Son

STERLING INNOVATION
An imprint of Sterling Publishing Co., Inc.

New York / London
www.sterlingpublishing.com

10 9 8 7 6 5 4

This 2009 edition published by Sterling Innovation, by arrangement with The Book Shop, Ltd.

Sterling Publishing Co., Inc.
387 Park Avenue South, New York, NY 10016

Book and origami papers designed by Kyung-Ah Son

This book is part of the *Fabulous Folded Flowers* kit and is not to be sold separately.

Printed and bound in China

Sterling ISBN 978-1-4351-0960-5

Table of Contents

Folding Tips

* Look through all the instructions for a given model before starting to fold.

* The pictures will tell most of the story. The text just fills in some details. Get used to reading both pictures and words together.

* Don't use the printed papers to make your first attempts. Practice on plain origami paper or trimmed scraps of wrapping paper before making the final models on the special papers.

* Generally, origami requires sharp, precise folds. But since flowers have a more organic flow, it's OK for origami flowers to have slightly irregular folds, too.

Key to Symbols

Whoever coined the phrase "a picture is worth a thousand words" must have had origami in mind. Throughout this book, we've used set symbols to stand in for words wherever it is most convenient. We've also used some set terms that are specific to the art of origami.

Dashed line = valley fold
Fold sides together to make a v shape

Broken dashed line = mountain fold
Fold sides together to make a ʌ shape

This is the patterned side.

This is the gradated side.

Preliminary Base

This basic shape is used in many of the origami flower models.

1 Position the paper so that the patterned side is face down.

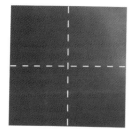 

2 Valley fold the paper in half horizontally and vertically. Unfold after each fold.

3 Mountain fold the paper in half along both diagonals, unfolding after each fold.

4 Turn the paper over. Then push two opposite sides together and flatten the model.

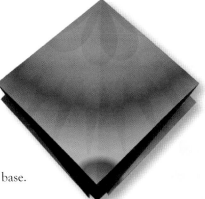

This is the completed preliminary base.

Magenta Bellflower

1 Position the paper so that the patterned side is face down. Valley fold the paper on the diagonal so that it not quite in half.

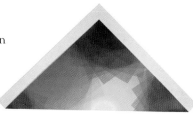

2 Valley fold the model in half along the dashed line.

3 Pull the inner tip (point A) down about a third of the way down the model and flatten.

A

4 Overlap the two ends to make a cone.

5 Mountain fold and valley fold the excess over the edge of the model to lock the cone in place.

An inside view of the finished flower.

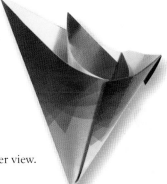

The finished flower, outer view.

Indigo Poppy

1 Position the paper so the patterned side is face down. Make an off-center valley fold as shown.

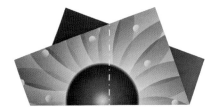

2 Now mountain fold the model in half and unfold.

3 Make two mountain folds to the center crease as shown. Then fold the model in half.

4 Mountain fold the top layer as shown. This will make a little latch.

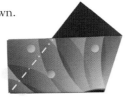 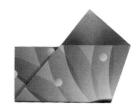

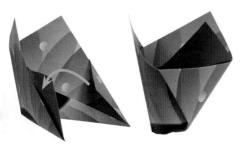

5 Now curl the bottom corner around to the front and latch it onto the outer edge of the model.

6 Inside the flower, press the center flat.

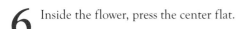

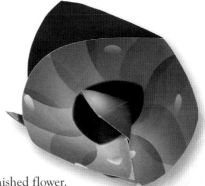

The finished flower.

Pink Foamflower

1 Position the paper so that the patterned side is face down. Valley fold in half horizontally and vertically. Mountain fold along the diagonals. Unfold after each fold.

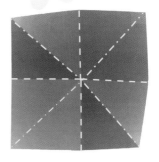

2 Fold each corner in part of the way.

3 Mountain fold one of the corners in half, matching points A and B to make a flap.

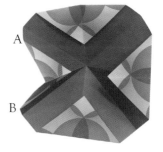

A

B

4 Holding the flap, spiral it inward, folding the top edge over to anchor it.

5 Curl back the outer edge of the model.

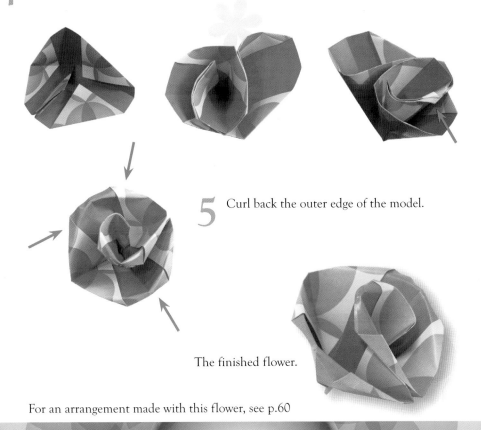

The finished flower.

For an arrangement made with this flower, see p.60

13

Orange Sunburst

1 Position the paper so the patterned side is face up.

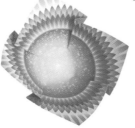

2 Grab the edge of the paper between your thumb and forefinger and pull to the left. Repeat on the other three sides of the model.

3 Fold some of the excess between the petals underneath to lock the petal in place.

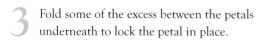

4 Turn the model over. Pressing up from underneath, form the center point into a little tip. Give it a bit of a twist.

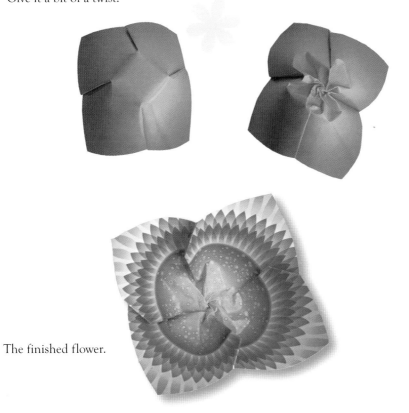

The finished flower.

Golden Trollius

1 Make a preliminary base (see p. 6).

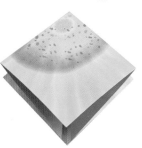

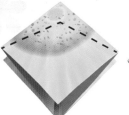
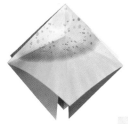

2 Fold the top layer along the dashed lines and pull the bottom point up.

3 Repeat on the other three sides, then turn the model over.

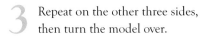

4 Grab the center folds and twist to the left. Flatten at the outer edges. Then pull the edge at point A over to the left, valley folding along the dashed lines. Repeat with other three folds.

A

5 Turn the model over. Fold the petal corners under to lock each in place.

6 Turn the model back over and fold back the petal tips. Then fold back the corners of the tips to make the petals rounder.

The finished model.

Blushing Heart

1. Position the paper so the patterned side is face up. Then valley fold the paper horizontally and vertically. Unfold.

2. Valley fold the model again, a little below the horizontal fold and a little to the right of the vertical. Then, mountain fold along diagonals as shown.

3. Use the creases as your folding guide to fold the model into this shape.

4 Fold the edges of the top square to the center crease. Unfold.

5 Pull the top point of the upper layer out and flatten. Fold down both sides as shown.

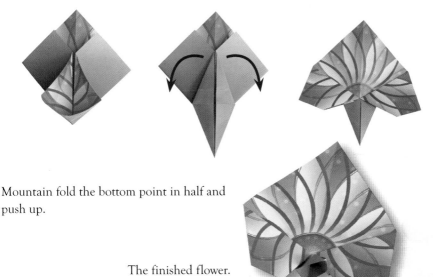

6 Mountain fold the bottom point in half and push up.

The finished flower.

Wild Bergamot

1 Make a preliminary base (see p. 6).

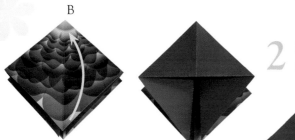

2 Fold the top layer up, matching point A to point B. Repeat for the other three sides.

3 Make an inside reverse fold (mountain fold the top layer along the center crease and pull down).

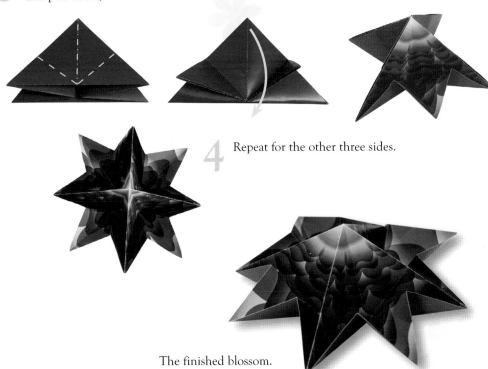

4 Repeat for the other three sides.

The finished blossom.

Ruffle-Edged Tulip

1   Make a preliminary base (see p. 6). Fold the edges of the top layer to the center crease.

2   Unfold. Pull the layer out and up.

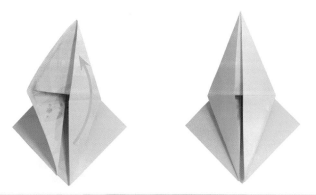

3 Turn the model over and repeat on the other side. Fold the top layer down one side at a time. Rotate the model 180°.

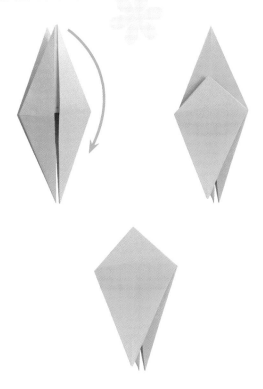

Make two little flaps at the corners, one folded in and one folded back. Then turn
the model over and repeat on the other side.

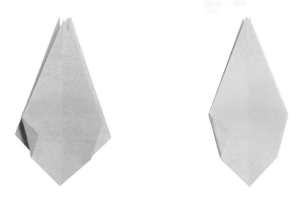

Pull the layers open gently.

6 Open a petal; spread the edges apart with a finger and flatten. Repeat with the other petals.

7 Curl the tops of each petal a bit to the outside.

The finished blossom.

Sunrise Primrose

1 Turn the paper so that the patterned side is face up. Then make valley folds along the diagonals and mountain folds horizontally and vertically.

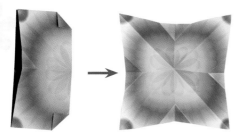

2 After making the vertical fold, fold down the two upper corners. Repeat after folding horizontally. Then, unfold the model and reposition patterned side up. Use your finger to press the fold inward as shown. Repeat with other three sides.

3 Bring the corners of a petal together and fold excess over to make edges between petals. Repeat with all other petals.

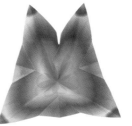 

4 Fold some of the excess under again to lock each petal in place.

5 Turn the model over. Gently press the center point inward to make a rounded flower center.

6 Turn the model back over. With the thumb and forefinger, gently press in on the edges of a petal to give it a ruffly shape.

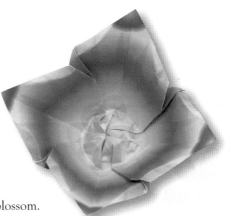

The finished blossom.

Feathered Phlox

1   Make a preliminary base (see p. 6) with gradated side out. Fold the top point down.

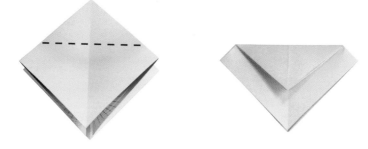

2   Open up the model and flatten. Mountain fold the creases in the center to make a square.

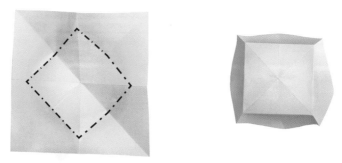

3 Use a finger to press the center point down, then press two opposite sides of the square into the center.

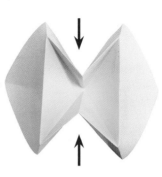

4 Now flatten the model.

5 On the top layer, make an inside reverse fold (mountain fold along the center crease and pull down to the bottom edge of the model).

6 Repeat with the other three sides. Then insert a finger into the center of the model from below and push up to round.

7 Fold the points between the petals together and tuck out of sight.

8 Fold the tip of each petal back. Then fold back the corners of each tip to make the petals more round.

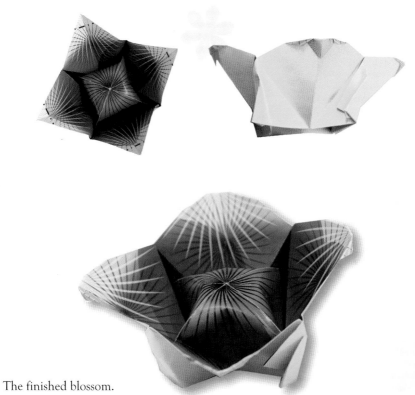

The finished blossom.

Shooting Star

1. Position the paper so the patterned side is face up. Mountain fold in half horizontally and vertically. Valley fold along the diagonals. Unfold after each fold.

2. Push two opposite sides inward, collapsing the model as shown. Valley fold along the dashed lines shown.

3. Repeat on other three sides, then turn the model over.

4 Flatten the center part of the model; press the middle to the right as shown.

5 Turn the model back over and open up the petals.

The finished flower.

For an arrangement made with this flower, see p.63

Lavender Daylily

1 Make a preliminary base (see p. 6) with the patterned side out.

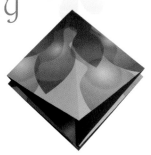

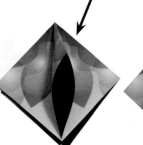

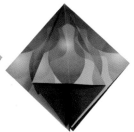

2 Turn one of the flaps like a page; squash it flat.

3 Repeat with other three flaps.

Fold the bottom edges to the center crease. Unfold.

Fold the tip down and unfold. Pull the edge at point A up.

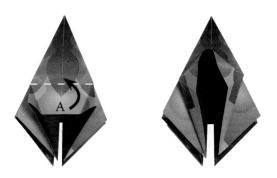

6 Flatten and repeat on other sides. Rotate the model 180° and fold point A up, repeating on all sides.

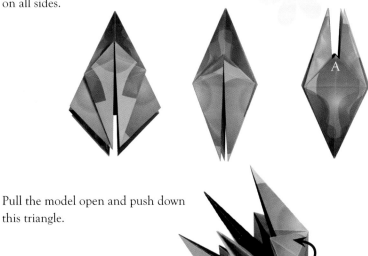

7 Pull the model open and push down this triangle.

8 Push the triangle against the inside of the model and flatten. Repeat on all sides.

9 Turn the top left flap over like a page. Turn the model over and repeat. Then, fold the bottom edges into the center crease; repeat on all sides.

10 Pull the model open; push the corners between the petals down as shown.

The finished flower.

For an arrangement made with this flower, see p.61

Golden Starflower

1 Position the paper so that the patterned side is face up. Valley fold in half horizontally and vertically. Mountain fold along the diagonals. Unfold.

2 Fold each corner into the center.

3 Fold each corner back out three quarters of the way.

4 Valley fold along the dashed lines shown.

5 Mountain fold the creases between the valley folds. Alternating valley and mountain folds, push the model into this diamond shape. Fold the top point down and unfold.

6 Open the model back up and turn it over. Mountain fold over the creases around the center point.

7 Use your finger to press the center point down, then push two opposite sides together, pleating until it lies flat.

8 Mountain fold the top layer along the center crease, then pull the point down to make valley folds as shown. Flatten to make a petal. Repeat to make four large petals with points in between.

9 Push down the points between the large petals to make smaller petals.

10 Pushing up from underneath, gently round the flower center.

The finished flower.

Violet Hyacinth

1. Position the paper so that the patterned side is face down. Valley fold in half horizontally and vertically. Mountain fold along the diagonals. Unfold after each fold.

2. Fold each corner to the center point.

3. Fold each corner back out three quarters of the way.

4 Valley fold along the dashed lines shown. Unfold.

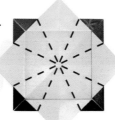 

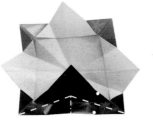

5 Unfold two of the corners back to the center point. Bring up the bottom edge, valley folding to the center crease, matching the two white dots. Repeat on the other side of the bottom edge. Mountain fold the center crease.

6 Rotate the model 180° and repeat on the opposite side.

7 Valley fold along the dashed lines where indicated, then press in with a finger to mountain fold in between. Then mountain fold along the broken dashed lines in white where indicated.

8 Pleating the model along alternating mountain and valley folds, fold it down and flatten. Valley fold the lower right edge so the top layer is flush with the bottom layers. Turn the model over and repeat on the other side.

9 Fold down the top layer and flatten to make the first petal.

10 Fold down and flatten the remaining petals, overlapping them a little as you rotate the model. Make little folds at the base to allow you to fan out the petals.

11 Curl each petal tip by rolling around a pencil.

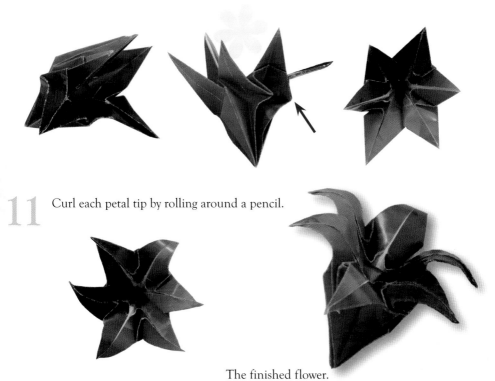

The finished flower.

For an arrangement made with this flower, see p.64

Blazing Star

1. Position the paper so that the patterned side is face down. Valley fold in half horizontally and vertically. Mountain fold along the diagonals. Unfold after each fold.

2. Fold each corner into center point.

3. Fold each corner back out three quarters of the way.

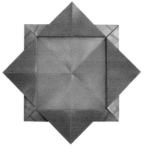

4 Valley fold the model along the dashed lines as indicated, unfolding after making each fold.

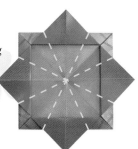

5 Pleating the model along alternating mountain and valley folds, fold it down and flatten. Fold the top point down and unfold.

6 Unfold entire model. Position as shown below. Mountain fold the creases around the center point.

7 Push the center point down with a finger while pleating the center until the model collapses.

8 Flatten the model. Mountain fold the top layer along the center crease, then pull the point out to make the valley folds indicated. Repeat on remaining three large petals (there are four large ones and four small ones).

9 Spread out five petals (four large, one small). Pinch three of the center pleats closed to make five main sides for the flower center.

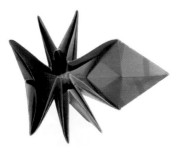

10 Turn the model over. The remaining three petals will be visible as points sticking up. Fold them down and tuck out of sight.

11 Turn the model back over. Close up the pleats, folding them down to anchor.

The finished flower.

For an arrangement made with this flower, see p.62

Greenery

Choose from this selection of leaves and stems to make your finished flower models.

Broad Leaf

1 Position the paper so the patterned side is face down. Valley fold along the dashed line shown.

2 Valley fold the opposite corner, overlapping the first folded side slightly.

3 Valley fold the shorter sides into the center of the model.

4 Now valley fold the model in half. This is one version of the finished leaf.

5 To make a broad leaf with a stem, valley fold the base as shown, then push the tip up, between the two halves of the leaf.

The finished leaf.

Speckled Leaf

1 Place the paper so the patterned side is face down. Valley fold two opposite corners into the center.

2 Valley fold the corners along dashed lines shown, to make the leaf rounder.

3 Valley fold the model in half. If you like, add a small dab of glue at one end between the layers to help it stay shut.

The finished leaf.

Spiky Fronds

1 Using the paper shown, draw long, skinny triangles—the bases should be ¼ inch to ½ inch wide. Cut them out.

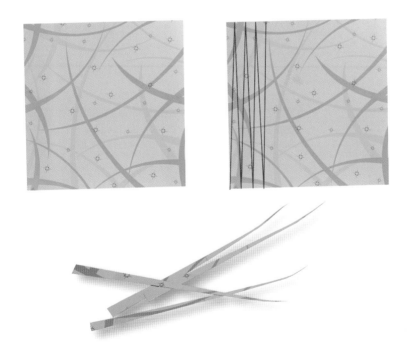

Jungle Palm

1. Position the paper so the patterned side is face down. Valley fold along the dashed lines shown.

2. Valley fold the shorter sides along the dashed lines shown.

3. Valley fold the base, then mountain fold it back part of the way to make a zigzag fold. This will be the stem.

4 Fold the edges of the stem into the center crease

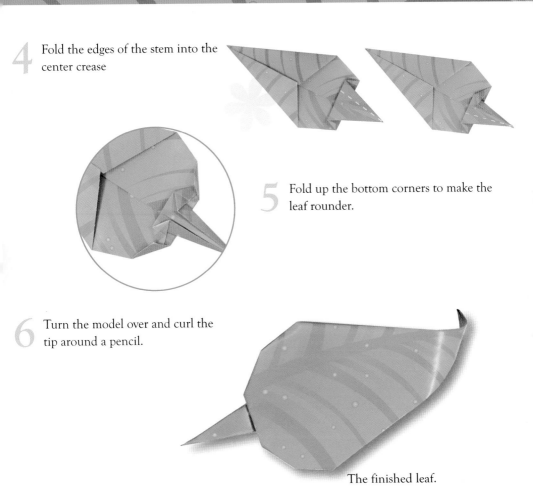

5 Fold up the bottom corners to make the leaf rounder.

6 Turn the model over and curl the tip around a pencil.

The finished leaf.

Use instant grab, fast-drying glue so the drying time will take only a few moments.

Reinforced Flower Stem

These will support large and/or heavy blossoms.

1   Cut long strips about 1 inch wide. Glue two strips together at one edge to make a strip long enough for a stem. Allow to dry.

2   Fold one edge in part way, then fold the opposite edge in, overlapping the first.

3   Unfold. Fold a piece of floral stem wire to the same length. Insert between the layers. Glue the stem shut. Allow to dry.

Wire-Free Flower Stem

Stems without the reinforcement of wire are good for more compact blossoms.

1 Cut a long rectangle about 2 inches wide.
Fold it in half lengthwise.

2 Fold it in half lengthwise again.

3 Fold it half lengthwise one last time. Dab
with instant grab-fast dry glue along its
length to keep it closed.

Arrangements

Making the flowers is just half the fun. The other half is putting the blossoms, the stems and the leaves together to make fantastic flowers and one-of-a-kind arrangements. Here is what you'll need to assemble fabulous origami floral arrangements.

- Containers for the arrangements (vases, pots, glasses)

- Florist's foam or other vase fillers, such as pebbles or marbles

- Floral stem wire

- Black construction paper

- Instant grab, fast-drying glue

How to Attach a Flower to a Stem

Gather a folded stem and a finished flower model. Dab the stem with a bit of glue, find a likely flat spot on the outside of the flower, and press the flower to the stem. If the flower is cone-shaped or has folds, you can insert the stem into the base before you glue. In either case, you will have to hold it in place for a minute or so, until the glue sets.

Decide which leaves you want for your stem. Some, like the broad leaf or the spiky frond, don't have to be glued to the flower—you can insert them directly into the container when you insert your stems. Others can be glued directly onto the stem as outlined above.

Pink Foamflowers in a Glass Vase

1 Assemble 10 reinforced stems and flowers. Valley fold one tip on
each stem as shown.

2 One stem at a time, dab glue inside the valley-folded tips and press a flower
in place.

3 Fold 10 broad leaves with stems and glue in place, one on each stem.

4 Place finished stems in a clear glass vase, bending them slightly to give them
a natural look.

5 Arrange the stems so that
the flowers drape in
different directions.

Lots of Lilies

1 Assemble and glue 12 flowers with reinforced stems: when preparing thereinforced stems, leave one tip per stem unglued at the top. Then glue the tipsof each flower in between the folds at the tip of each stem.

2 Make 10 broad leaves.

3 Curl the base of a leaf around the stem of an assembled flower, then place them in a clear glass vase. Repeat with the rest of the finished stems and leaves. If you have more leaves than stems, just place the leaves where you like. In this arrangement, we used a glass container, which looks good filled with marbles.

4 Bend the stems slightly to give them a natural look.

5 Arrange the stems so that the flowers drape in different directions.

A Spray of Blazing Stars

Choose a long and narrow open-topped glass vase for this arrangement.

1 Make an extra-long stem by gluing four long stem strips together before folding. Reinforce with floral stem wire.

2 Make two regular-length, non-reinforced stems. Cut them into a total of eight shorter pieces, each 2–3 inches in length.

3 Glue the short stem pieces to eight flowers. Curl each stem a bit.

4 Make 10 broad leaves; insert them directly into the vase—no foam or other filler needed.

5 Insert the long stem among the leaves, making sure it is wedged firmly in place. Shape the stem a bit to give it a graceful, gentle curve.

6 Starting from the top of the long stem and working your way down, glue the short stems in place. Use as few or as many of the flowers as you like.

Shooting Stars in a Vase

1 Assemble and glue six flowers with reinforced stems.

2 Cut out 12–15 spiky fronds. Crumple them a little, if you like.

3 Place the florist's foam in the container, cutting or shaving it to fit if necessary.

4 Insert the stems into the foam, bending the stems to give them a natural look. Adjust the stems so that the flowers drape in different directions.

5 Fill out the arrangement with as many spiky fronds as you like, inserted into the foam.

6 When you like the arrange-ment, cover the foam with origami sand, made from torn bits of black construction paper, rolled up into little balls.

Potted Hyacinth

1 Place the florist's foam in the container, cutting it to fit if necessary. Make one reinforced stem. Leave some wire visible at the bottom, looped up. This will keep the stem from rotating. Insert into the foam.

2 Make 12 hyacinth blossoms.

3 Dab glue on the tip of one blossom and insert between the layers at the top of the stem. Press and allow to dry.

4 One at a time, dab glue on the tips of the remaining blossoms, affix to the stem and allow to dry. Blossoms at the top should tilt up. Blossoms in the middle should be level. Blossoms at the bottom should tilt down. Make sure each blossom is set before proceeding to the next.

5 Make eight broad leaves. Insert into the foam around the stem.

6 Cover the foam with origami sand (see p. 63).